AN

Ark

FOR

Today's Flood

by

CATHERYNE WOOD

AN

Ark

FOR

Today's Flood

by

CATHERYNE WOOD

BLAZE
PUBLISHING
Memphis, Tenn.

AN ARK FOR TODAY'S FLOOD

by Catheryne Wood

Published by Blaze Publishing House
P.O. Box 184
Mansfield, Texas
www.blazepublishinghouse.com

Cover Art Work by Michael Butler

ISBN-13: 978-0-9792071-8-1
ISBN-10: 0-9792071-8-5

Printed in the United States of America

Today's Flood:

Great Darkness, Deception, and Many Turbulent Waters

Ungodly rivers are overflowing and God has said, *"My people are destroyed for lack of knowledge."*

Hosea 4:6 (KJV)

God's Ark is our safe place in a troubled and violent world.

Dedication

I dedicate this book, first of all, to Jesus, my Lord and Savior, who instructed me to write these words.

And to all my children and grandchildren, for whom I continue to build God's Ark.

Acknowledgments

S pecial thanks to Michael Butler for the "Noah's Ark" book cover design.

Naida Johnson, RN, CWS, FCCWS, for special editing.

Joan Hunter, of Joan Hunter International Ministries, for special encouragement.

Table of Contents

Foreword

GOD TOLD NOAH TO BUILD AN ARK
FOR HIS DAY.

HE IS TELLING US TO BUILD AN ARK
FOR OUR DAY.

We are on the brink of the greatest outpouring of the Spirit of God the world has ever known. But, at the same time, a satanic flood is being poured out as never before.

Just as God told Noah how to prepare an Ark which would save his household from the flood of his day, He is telling us how to prepare an Ark which would save our households from the flood of our day.

Preface

This book was written in obedience to God's desire that His people be protected in the midst of all the evil deception and violence being loosed on the earth in this end time.

With much of the world now reeling in confusion and uncertainty, the Lord spoke this into my spirit: *"This is now BOTH seed time and harvest time."* I was immediately reminded of Amos 9:13:

> *"Behold, the days are coming,' says the LORD, 'When the plowman shall overtake the reaper, and the treader of grapes him who sows seed; the mountains shall drip with sweet wine, and all the hills shall flow with it.'"*

God is a God of plan and purpose, and what He has spoken will come to pass. The fearful "Day of the Lord" is fast approaching. He clearly states that when He re-gathers His people, the Jews, back into their own land, He will then gather all nations and bring them down into the Valley of Jehoshaphat (the "valley of decision") for judgment. There the nations will be judged for how they have treated His chosen people—for scattering Israel among the nations, and for parting the land God gave them (Joel 3).

This does not mean He loves Israel more than other nations, but He chose them to bring forth the Messiah, Jesus, to be Savior of the world. Even though Israel failed to recognize Him as their Messiah, Zechariah 2:8 says whoever touches Israel touches the apple of God's eye. He will never forget His chosen people.

"But Judah will be inhabited forever, and Jerusalem for all generations. And I will avenge their blood which I have not avenged, for the LORD dwells in Zion."

Joel 3:20-21 (NASB)

God is already gathering the nations to the Valley of Jehoshaphat for judgment. We have only to look at the daily world news concerning Israel. There are still some events which have to occur, but the pieces of the puzzle are falling into place at an ever-increasing pace. It is as if God has shifted gears, and the wheels are turning faster and faster.

As the rivers of this end-time satanic flood continue to rise, I pray you will be safely preserved in God's Ark.

Introduction

"But as the days of Noe were, so shall also the coming of the Son of man be. For as in the days that were before the flood they were eating and drinking, marrying and giving in marriage, until the day that Noe entered into the ark, and knew not until the flood came, and took them all away; so shall also the coming of the Son of man be."

Matthew 24:37-39 (KJV)

The earth today is in chaos, almost as it was in the days of Noah, and there is a flood—a flood from Satan, our enemy. This flood has many rivers feeding it: rivers of deception, lies, and misrepresentations. It's a flood filled with words, pictures, evil reports, intimidations, and actions which mislead, entice, and appeal to the lust of the flesh, lust of the eyes, and the pride of life; and where fears abound.

We have wars, earthquakes, floods, hurricanes, famines, drought, AIDs, economic upheaval, poverty, racial unrest, and divisions. These are all anti-godly tributaries feeding the flood which keep our eyes on the problems, instead of on the problem-solver—God.

Deception and fear are tools of the enemy, and this river of deception is not *coming*, it is already here. It continues to rise and cover the earth. The current is getting stronger and stronger and it surrounds us on every side, in every direction we look, and in much of what we hear.

> *"And the serpent cast out of his mouth water as a flood after the woman, that he might cause her to be carried away of the flood."*

Revelation 12:15 (KJV)

What comes out of the mouth? Words! Satan is the father of lies and a polished deceiver. He is working furiously to deceive everyone he can, for he knows his time is very short.

We have reached the time prophesied by Jesus Christ almost 2,000 years ago.

> *"And there will be signs in the sun, in the moon, and in the stars; and on the earth distress of nations, with perplexity, the sea and the waves roaring; men's hearts failing them from fear and the expectation of those things which are coming on the earth, for the powers of heaven will be shaken."*

Luke 21:25-26

However, Jesus did not leave us hanging. In the midst of these frightening events, He also gave us hope when He said:

"Now when these things begin to happen, look up and lift up your heads, because your redemption draws near."

Luke 21:28

Noah was warned by God about things which would come in the future. The state of his world *then* also describes our present world situation. The Word of God warns us of events we have not yet seen, nor can we scarcely imagine.

Noah believed God and started building the Ark. The long ride in the Ark was not a honeymoon trip or a vacation. The Ark was a lifeboat which saved Mankind from total destruction. God brought Noah and his family safely through.

This is a beautiful foreshadow of the "secret place of the Most High" (Psalms 91:1) and the Ark of refuge which Jesus offers you and me. He offers us shelter from the storms of life. He will carry us through the flood waters we face and provide protection from the elements of sin. He offers us provision for body, soul, and spirit.

But, as with Noah, He expects us to believe and start building.

Chapter 1

GOD STILL SPEAKS

One day my niece was having a big conversation with her five year-old son, Alex. Suddenly, Alex looked at his mother and asked, "Does God talk to you?" She answered, "Well, yes, He does."

Then Alex asked her, "Why don't I hear Him?"

She tried to explain, "God speaks to my heart."

Little Alex thought about it for a minute. Then his eyes lit up as he said, "Oh, I see! God talks to your heart, then it goes up here,"—pointing to his head—"and you think about it."

Out of the mouth of babes!

The simple truth is that God will speak to all who trust and walk close to Him; and it is an awesome and thrilling experience every time.

Faith

H ebrews 11 is sometimes referred to as the "faith chapter." I have read it many times, but in studying it one day, I came to verse seven:

> *"By faith Noah, being divinely warned of things not yet seen, moved with godly fear, prepared an ark for the saving of his household, by which he condemned the world and became heir of the righteousness which is according to faith."*

Hebrews 11:7

Suddenly, just as little Alex had understood, the Lord spoke very clearly to my heart:

> *"Build an Ark with My Word and your obedience for the saving of your house. Build it with* **My Word** *and* **your obedience.** *"*

Then my spirit was further impressed with these words:

> *"Not only will your house be blessed, but many others also."*

I paused to pray and meditate on these instructions, and then I continued reading:

"By faith Abraham, when he was called to go out into a place which he should after receive for an inheritance, obeyed; and he went out, not knowing whither he went."

"Through faith also Sara herself received strength to conceive seed, and was delivered of a child when she was past age, because she judged him faithful who had promised."

Hebrews 11:8, 11 (KJV)

Again, the Lord quickened my spirit as He gave me His instructions:

1. **"Build an Ark on My Word and your obedience— with a Noah-kind of faith."**

2. **"Obey Me even if you don't understand where I am leading you—with an Abraham-kind of faith."**

3. **"Conceive within yourself the seed of God's Truth—with a Sarah-kind of faith, and birth it and bring it forth, regardless of your age, because you judge Me faithful."**

In obedience, I have placed myself under the direction of the Holy Spirit to the building of this Ark, not knowing where all it will lead. I am trusting God to reveal His seed of Truth concerning this matter, and to bring it forth as He desires.

Be a willing vessel.

Chapter 2

NOAH

AN EXAMPLE OF COMMITMENT

S ometimes we can become so familiar with a subject that, in reading through it, we just sort of skim over it. But now that the Lord had instructed *me* to build an Ark, I knew I needed to do a more thorough study.

We are told that stories in the Old Testament are to be examples for us to learn from today. So, how can Noah and *his* Ark relate to our lives or show us what to do in *our* day? What could I learn that might apply to our present situation?

Noah, the Man

W hy was Noah chosen? How would he ever be able to successfully achieve the gigantic and seemingly impossible task God had assigned to him?

Noah's great-grandfather was Enoch, who pleased God and was translated to Heaven without seeing death. His grandfather was Methuselah, who lived the longest life ever recorded. Noah's father, Lamech, was a preacher. Obviously, Noah was raised among men who knew God. 2 Peter 2:5 tells us that Noah was also a "preacher of righteousness."

Other than his birth, we find nothing about Noah's early days except that his name means "comfort."

"And he called his name Noah, saying, This same shall comfort us concerning our work and toil of our hands, because of the ground which the LORD hath cursed."

Genesis 5:29 (KJV)

The Bible teaches that the descendants of the righteous are blessed. Genesis 6 tells us Noah both walked with God and found grace in the eyes of the Lord. So, we can certainly agree that Noah was a man of God.

In those days, men usually lived hundreds of years, and Genesis 5:32 says Noah was 500 years old and the father of three sons: Shem, Ham, and Japheth.

Japheth became the ancestor of the Indo-European peoples known as Gomer, Magog, Tubal, and Meshech. Shem became the ancestor of the Hebrews, and Ham was the father of the Canaanite tribes. All nations in the earth today are descendants from Japheth, Shem, or Ham (Genesis 9:19). However, it was through Shem that God planned for the Messiah to come. "Shem" simply means "name." From Shem comes the One who bears the name which is above ALL names—Jesus!

World of Wickedness

But in Noah's day, God saw the great wickedness of Man. The imaginations and thoughts of Man were continually evil. The Lord's heart was grieved, and He was sorry He had ever made Man on the earth.

"So the LORD said, 'I will destroy man whom I have created from the face of the earth, both man and beast, creeping thing and birds of the air, for I am sorry that I have made them.'"

Genesis 6:7

God's Grace

However, Noah found grace in the eyes of the Lord because he was a just man and believed in God (Genesis 6:8-9). The Bible also says he was "perfect in his generations," meaning that he was of the proper lineage for the future birth of the Christ child.

Scripture tells us that God will not do anything until He first warns His prophets. So, God spoke to Noah:

"And God said to Noah, 'The end of all flesh has come before Me, for the earth is filled with violence through them; and behold, I will destroy them with the earth.'"

Genesis 6:13

Hearing God's audible voice is an awesome, unbelievable, and reverent experience. It is not to be taken lightly. Rather, we are compelled to take it very seriously. Noah heard God, and Hebrews 11:7 (KJV) says he was *"moved with fear."* This was not just a natural fear, but a Godly fear—a reverence toward God.

We know that Abraham is called the "father of faith," and rightly so. But Noah also had to have tremendous faith. Just think what a strange and—from a human standpoint—almost impossible task he was called to do. We have never really appreciated the immensity of his assignment.

It had never rained before the flood occurred and there were no great bodies of water on which to sail a huge boat. This Ark was something no one had ever seen before. As

Noah worked year after year, godless unbelievers would come to watch, laugh, and ridicule him. But in spite of the negative influence from the unbelievers who surrounded him, he maintained his faith, obeyed God, and continued building the Ark.

He was considered quite "mad" by most. Even though Noah's own family probably had doubts about his obsession, they were the only ones who supported him and, consequently, were the only ones ultimately allowed into the Ark. I wonder if his sons or their wives truly believed their father had heard correctly from God . . . until it started raining.

Only members of Noah's immediate family were saved, but take heart! God is true to ALL who believe His Word:

"So they said, 'Believe on the Lord Jesus Christ, and you will be saved, you and your household.'"

Acts 16:31

Yes, each one of our loved ones need to individually accept Jesus as their Savior and Lord, but God made His promises to *all* who believe.

"But Jesus looked at them and said to them, 'With men this is impossible, but with God all things are possible.'"

Matthew 19:26

Righteousness by Faith

Faith in God means you have complete, total confidence in God's Word. Considering Noah's surroundings, the magnitude of the work he was called upon to do, and the many years spent in hard labor accomplishing it without giving up, he stands extremely tall among the men of faith mentioned in the Bible. Hebrews chapter 11 tells us Noah became an heir of righteousness by his faith. He had stubborn faith!

Summary

Noah believed God. He had a reverent fear of his Heavenly Father. He was righteous (in "right-standing" with God through faith) and acted on that faith. He preached what God had told him, warning the people and speaking the Word of God year after year, even though they did not listen.

Noah persevered in spite of criticism, ridicule, and unbelief from others. He continued to focus on the word from the Lord and did not quit or give up. He kept pressing forward in total obedience.

There was no sign of God's impending judgment during the time Noah was building the Ark. Yet, true to His Word,

God's judgment suddenly fell—and the people who had rejected His warning were all destroyed.

Noah had not only heard, but believed! He became obedient by putting his faith into action. In spite of so much criticism, opposition, and the many years it took, he did not give up.

Victory was his!

Chapter 3

GOD'S INSTRUCTIONS FOR NOAH'S ARK

"Make yourself an ark of gopherwood; make rooms in the ark, and cover it inside and outside with pitch. And this is how you shall make it: The length of the ark shall be three hundred cubits, its width fifty cubits, and its height thirty cubits. You shall make a window for the ark, and you shall finish it to a cubit from above; and set the door of the ark in its side. You shall make it with lower, second, and third decks."

Genesis 6:14-16

What was the Ark? Physically, it was a very large seaworthy vessel, which was constructed on dry land. It was built of gopher wood, an unknown wood which may also have been known as the cypress of Assyria, which was later used in shipbuilding because it was not likely to rot or be eaten by worms.

Pitch

We are told that the Ark was covered both inside and outside with a substance called pitch. The word "pitch" is used twice in verse 14, but two different words were used in the original Hebrew translation.

The first occurrence of "pitch" is: "... *pitch it within* ..." Here, the word "pitch" uses the Hebrew word *kaphar* which means "to cover." This word *kaphar* was used 69 times in the Old Testament for the word "atonement." The covering of *kaphar* represents the blood of Jesus, for atonement comes only through Christ's shed blood.

The second occurrence of "pitch" is: "... *and without with pitch.*" Here, the word "pitch" uses the Hebrew word *kopher*, meaning "resin" or "sealant." Symbolically, this represents the sealing by the Holy Spirit.

Physically, the Ark was caulked, and then covered over with a coal or wood tar. This tar substance was found in the Babylonian area, where it was thought to have been used in building the Tower of Babel.

Spiritually, however, the Ark was covered supernaturally with the blood of Jesus and then sealed by the Holy Spirit.

God is Specific

G od gives specific instructions; He does not generalize. Noah was given exact dimensions so the Ark would stay afloat, even with the heavy weight of all the animals, people, and food which would be loaded aboard.

The size was to be 300 x 50 x 30 cubits. A "cubit" is generally considered to have been a measurement of 18 or 20 inches—the distance between a man's hand and his elbow.

Noah's Ark was about the size of today's large ocean liner. Keep in mind, nothing like this or of this magnitude had ever been built before. No scientists, seamen, or navigators were involved. God gave the instructions directly to Noah.

Dry Land

N oah built this unprecedented structure, God's Ark, on dry ground.

"Now the flood was on the earth forty days. The waters increased and lifted up the ark, and it rose high above the earth."

Genesis 7:17

Before The Flood, all lands were connected together in one vast block. The earth was not divided into continents and islands until after The Flood.

Genesis 10:32 tells us the nations—the people of the earth—were divided after The Flood according to the families and generations of the sons of Noah. Verse 25 says the earth was divided in the days of Peleg, which was the fifth generation after Noah, through his son, Shem.

Multitudes Filled the Earth

Before the Great Flood there were great multitudes of men on earth. The sons and daughters of Adam had started many branches of the human race. But only Seth's line of descendants is listed throughout this period. His seed was to bring forth the lineage of the Messiah from Adam to Christ.

God saw that the earth was filled with man's great wickedness and violence, and that all flesh had corrupted their way (Genesis 6:5-12). Noah, however, a just man, found grace in the eyes of the Lord.

The Mist

During this time, Genesis 2:6 tells us that all the earth was watered by a mist rising up from the ground. This indicates God had not sent rain upon the earth since the day He moved upon the waters (Genesis 1:2), when the earth was without form and full of darkness. Many believe that condition was probably the result of Lucifer (Satan) being thrown out of Heaven.

Since all vegetation was watered by a rising mist from the ground, we can conclude that the inhabitants of Noah's day had never seen rain or a flood of water. And here was this seemingly foolish old man, not only spending years of hard labor building a huge boat on dry land, but preaching that a flood was coming. A flood? Imagine how the people must have laughed, taunted, and mocked him.

But when God speaks, Man should listen. Noah had heard the awesome voice of God!

"So the LORD said, 'I will destroy man whom I have created from the face of the earth, both man and beast, creeping thing and birds of the air, for I am sorry that I have made them. . . . And behold, I Myself am bringing floodwaters on the earth, to destroy from under heaven all flesh in which is the breath of life; everything that is on the earth shall die.'"

Genesis 6:7, 17

One Week

W hen the preparation time was over and the Ark was finished, God gave Noah a week to load it with all its cargo. I believe God had already supernaturally gathered the animals and fowls for Noah. This was surely a confirmation that he had heard God correctly. He had seven days to load the animals, food stuff, and his family before the destructive rain and flood waters would begin.

These seven days correspond with God giving His Church "Seven Church Periods" to bring in the harvest before the "end-time" destruction will begin at the Tribulation. (I discussed this at length in my book, *Seven Letters From Jesus.*)

After those seven days—and on the *very same day* Noah finished loading the Ark with all the animals and his family— the rain began to fall. The flood came; God's judgment fell.

> *"So those that entered, male and female of all flesh, went in as God had commanded him; and the LORD shut him in."*

> **Genesis 7:16**

God Himself sealed Noah's Ark by a supernatural act. They were all safely sealed in and protected with provisions for their journey to an unknown destination.

This is an example of His Covenant with us. If we are shut in with Him in His Word and truly trust Him, He will seal us with His Holy Spirit and bless us with protection and provision.

Faith and Obedience

By Noah first hearing God's voice, believing what he heard and then obeying God's directions, the Ark became a place of safety for God's chosen remnant. By putting his faith into action, Noah's efforts became their haven from the coming storm. That Ark was God's appointed place to protect and provide for true Believers. It brought them through dangerous and troubled flood waters to dry land and safety.

God's promises are conditional upon faith and obedience. What if Noah had decided the task was too great, and the scorn and ridicule of his friends and neighbors too much?

He had to turn his back on the rest of the world and ignore the rejection and ridicule of his friends. Noah had to focus on the instructions and commands of the Lord and ignore the worldly opinions of men.

Noah decided he believed God. He feared God more than the threats and insults of the people.

Summary

God is specific! His instructions may not make much sense and may even seem foolish, but they are to be faithfully and obediently followed, regardless of opposition and criticism.

Never alter His plans or give up, no matter how difficult the labor, or how long it takes.

Whatever God says, the decision to obey is up to us. He gives us the choice. He will not force us or demand our obedience or love. We see, we hear, we examine, and we ponder His Word—and in the end, we always have a free choice to accept Him or reject Him.

Fulfillment and timing are in God's hands, and there is always victory in Him. Noah made the right choice and went on to ultimate victory.

We all make our own choices. Will we walk in victory with God's perfect guidance and will?

What is your choice?

Chapter 4

THE GREAT FLOOD

G od was so grieved with the corrupt wickedness of Man that He sent a flood to destroy them.

"Then the LORD saw that the wickedness of man was great in the earth, and that every intent of the thoughts of his heart was only evil continually. And the LORD was sorry that He had made man on the earth, and He was grieved in His heart. So the LORD said, 'I will destroy man whom I have created from the face of the earth, both man and beast, creeping thing and birds of the air, for I am sorry that I have made them.' But Noah found grace in the eyes of the LORD."

Genesis 6:5-8

We are told in 1 Peter 3:20 that the divine, long suffering of God waited in the days of Noah while the Ark was being prepared—where only a few (8) souls were saved through The Flood.

After The Great Flood had accomplished its purpose, God made a covenant with Noah, with his seed after him, and with all living creatures for perpetual generations. He promised Man that He would never again destroy all living things by a flood of water. He set His rainbow in the clouds as a token of that covenant.

> *"'And as for Me, behold, I establish My covenant with you and with your descendants after you, and with every living creature that is with you: the birds, the cattle, and every beast of the earth with you, of all that go out of the ark, every beast of the earth. Thus I establish My covenant with you: Never again shall all flesh be cut off by the waters of the flood; never again shall there be a flood to destroy the earth.' And God said: 'This is the sign of the covenant which I make between Me and you, and every living creature that is with you, for perpetual generations: I set My rainbow in the cloud, and it shall be for the sign of the covenant between Me and the earth. It shall be, when I bring a cloud over the earth, that the rainbow shall be seen in the cloud; and I will remember My covenant which is between Me and you and every living creature of all flesh; the waters shall never again become a flood to destroy all flesh. The rainbow shall be in the cloud, and I will look on it to remember the everlasting covenant between God and every living creature of all flesh that is on the earth.' And God said to Noah, 'This is the sign of the covenant which I have established between Me and all flesh that is on the earth.'"*

Genesis 9:9-17

What a powerful promise! A covenant of His promise which the whole world can see every time it rains!

In 2 Peter 3, however, God declares He will again purge the earth of evil in the last days—but the NEXT time will be by fire.

Promised Seed

G od is always true to His Word. He made a promise in Genesis 3:15 that a "Seed" would come forth of the woman, Eve, who would crush the head of the serpent. He needed to preserve the Adamic line (heritage).

God is a God of plan and purpose, and Noah, who was of the proper lineage for the future birth of the Christ child, was preserved. Thus, the Seed (Christ) came through Eve to crush the enemy (Satan). God's promise was fulfilled.

Decision Time

J ust as these last days are times of decision, they are also times of division for Mankind. Some people will rise to the highest heaven; others will be deceived, make wrong decisions, procrastinate, or reject the Gospel. Sadly, they will descend into the depths of hell. Contrary to what some believe, the Bible says hell is a real place.

We must commit ourselves fully to total obedience to God's Word. It is either all or nothing! It is either white or black! There is no gray area or straddling the fence. We are to follow Him unconditionally in every area of our lives. Deception is running rampant and everything will come to full maturity during these last of the Last Days.

Is salvation hard? It was for Jesus. It cost Him everything. God's price for sin is death, and only blood can pay that price. The blood of bulls and rams was only a temporary covering which had to be repeated over and over throughout the Old Testament.

Our Savior willingly shed His own blood. He laid down His own life and paid the full price for us. It was a terrible price—a shameful and painful death on an ugly cross with total separation from God, His Father. He did this just for us and went in our place. This ultimate price was paid so we could be redeemed back to our Father from the "fall" of Mankind through the sin of Adam and Eve.

"Greater love has no one than this, than to lay down one's life for his friends."

John 15:13

After God's only Son was crucified and buried in the tomb, He descended into the depths of Hades (hell) to get the keys to hell and the grave. He fought the battle for us, defeating Satan and his demonic bondage over mankind. He arose victorious. Death could not hold Him. He is alive forevermore!

Jesus is His Name. He is the Word of God (John 1:1, 14)! He laid down His life to become a "living" Ark for us; an Ark which will lift us out of bondage and carry us above the flood waters of sin, death, and all the evils of this world. Jesus is now seated at the right hand of God, the Father. I call that being God's "right-hand Man"!

A New Covenant Ark

The only entrance into this new covenant Ark is through Jesus, who is not only the Son of God, but also God's express Word. He will not force Himself on anyone, but waits for us to ask Him into our heart—to not only be our Savior, but also our Lord.

Then, through faith and obedience to His commandments, we have access to ALL the promises of God! But we have to believe them, claim them, and walk in them. This also means we must stand against the lies of the devil who continuously tries to stop us from receiving those wonderful promises.

God is waiting for us to enter into the new covenant Ark. Using the promises in His Word, we must build and surround ourselves and our households with the Ark which Jesus has provided for us.

Seek Him First

When you are dealing with God, you are dealing with the most powerful Being imaginable. He is all-powerful and all-knowing. All things are open before Him. He knows us better than we know ourselves—even our darkest secrets.

He tells us to seek Him first and foremost, and all the things we have need of will be added unto us (see Matthew 6:33). We must not let hindering forces hold us back. He also says to stay out of the "briar patch," where the Seed (His Word) gets choked by the cares of this world. I have been guilty of being caught in the "briars" and have experienced His reprimand. Thank the Lord we can repent, be restored, and be reconciled back to our loving Father's arms.

Today's Instant Society

In this day of instant this and instant that, we feel we have outgrown the simple basic truths. We think we are beyond that. We want the exciting things! We want miracles, gifts of the Spirit, and prophecies—and, yes, we should. We are told to desire the best gifts. But, they do not come if our foundation is cracked and crumbling. We must constantly guard against distractions which can creep in to get our focus off of God's Word and His plan for our lives. We have to stay focused in spite of our "busyness."

No one can deny that we are, indeed, in the end times, where many run to and fro and knowledge has increased (Daniel 12:4). But the enemy would like to keep us so busy that we do not have time for the things of God. Many times it is necessary to be a "busy Martha," but we must also choose to make time, pull aside, and be a "Mary" sitting at the feet of Jesus (Luke 10:38-42).

Back to the Basics

God has been impressing on me for several years that the Church has gone through many different phases and stages through the centuries of church development. Some of the basics have been neglected and forgotten. Unfortunately, many people are obsessed with the rules and opinions of men. Words of advice and guidance from important men of the world are now considered by many to be more important than THE Word, Jesus.

It is in Him that we live, move, and have our being (Acts 17:28). From Him we draw our strength, direction, and the purpose for which we have been created. Through Him we receive victory, fulfillment, peace, and joy.

We must get back to His basic teachings. God firmly planted these words in my spirit:

Come and sit at the feet of Jesus and learn from the Master what the Spirit is saying to the churches.

Chapter 5

GOD'S INSTRUCTIONS FOR OUR ARK

Today, we don't need to build a huge vessel of timber and pitch. God has already provided an Ark for us. It is an Ark built without hands—a spiritual Ark.

". . . I have called you by your name; you are Mine. When you pass through the waters, I will be with you; and through the rivers, they shall not overflow you. When you walk through the fire, you shall not be burned, nor shall the flame scorch you. For I am the Lord your God, the Holy One of Israel, your Savior . . ."

Isaiah 43:1b-3a

Better Promises

Our new Ark contains a new covenant with even better promises than the old covenant God made with Abraham

(Hebrews 8-10). This new covenant is not written on tablets of stone, but His commandments and laws are written on our hearts and in our minds.

Isaiah talks about this new covenant:

"'The Redeemer will come to Zion, And to those who turn from transgression in Jacob,' says the LORD. 'As for Me,' says the LORD, 'This is My covenant with them: My Spirit who is upon you, and My words which I have put in your mouth, shall not depart from your mouth, nor from the mouth of your descendants, nor from the mouth of your descendants' descendants,' says the LORD, 'from this time and forevermore.'"

Isaiah 59:20-21

Jesus is our High Priest. Through His Name and faith in His completed work at the cross, we can now enter directly into the throne room of God. He will receive us just the way we are—filthy rags and all. He will cleanse us, and then lovingly mold each of us into the person He created us to be.

Our Minds Have to be Renewed

Once we repent and accept Jesus as our Lord and Savior, the power of Satan over our life is broken; however, our minds still need to be "renewed." This renewing is a continual, daily process. We do not just automatically receive the mind of Christ; we must *choose* to become so saturated with His Word that our thoughts, attitudes, and desires are in obedience to Him. This should become heart knowledge—not just head knowledge—for faith comes from the heart.

> *"When you pass through the waters, I will be with you; and through the rivers, they shall not overflow you. When you walk through the fire, you shall not be burned, nor shall the flame scorch you."*

Isaiah 43:2

Jesus does not say we won't go through some difficult places; however, if we put our trust in Him, He promises to bring us through to victory. We will be elevated above the destruction and the defeat of this world.

Point of Our Strength

Most of us at some point have claimed the Word, stood on the Word, confessed the Word, and believed that it would come to pass for us—and it has! And it does! For God is a faithful God, and He watches over His Word to perform it.

But God says in 1 Peter 1:13 that we must gird up the loins of our minds. "Loins" refer to the most vital point of our strength. If our loins fail, then our body will fail. If the loins of our mind are weak, we will live in defeat.

We must build the Word—His Ark—around us like a hedge so strong and so tight and so sturdy that no temptation or crisis can alter our trust. Then, protected within that Ark, nothing can move us from our total commitment to Him. Doubt cannot enter our mind.

Just like Noah, we need to have faith to continue building (believing and standing) in spite of setbacks, opposition, persecution, distractions, or circumstances.

For our Ark to become strong, God's Word needs to become our way of life, deeply-rooted and part of our very being. Then God will seal us in with "pitch and tar." We are first sealed (sanctified) by the blood of the Lamb (Jesus), and then again sealed by God's Holy Spirit.

The Time is Now

The Lord says NOW is the time and NOW is the hour to enter completely and totally into the provision He has made for us. HIS WORD is ALL-POWER and ALL-TRUTH, and God has made it available to all who will receive Christ through faith and obedience. But it is up to us! We have a choice.

Yes, there is a cost. Salvation is free for the asking, but Jesus laid down His life for us and wants our total commitment in return. He bought us with a terrible price. How could we do less than commit our life back to Him in return? He has done all He is going to do. He has already accomplished everything we will ever need.

As He hung dying on the cross, He called out, "It is finished!" Now, it is up to us to enter into what He has provided. It is the secret place of the Most High spoken of in Psalm 91:1; and is not only for us, but for our entire household.

What a deal! He offers His love, care, strength, protection, and provision—and this includes health, safety, finances, job, and every other circumstance which affects our lives!

But we do have to make a choice—the choice to do our part. It does not just come to us automatically. We must do the believing, claiming, building, and expecting in spite of all the enemy will throw at us—and he will throw!

"Be sober, be vigilant; because your adversary the devil walks about like a roaring lion, seeking whom he may devour."

1 Peter 5:8

God's enemy, Satan, is also our enemy. Even though Jesus has defeated him, he still rules in the worldly affairs of men on this earth until Jesus returns. Satan goes around LIKE a roaring lion, devouring all who will fall for his lies and temptations. He is cunning and deceitful, but the Word says that when the enemy attacks, God's Holy Spirit steps in to protect us.

"When the enemy comes in like a flood, the Spirit of the LORD will lift up a standard against him."

Isaiah 59:19b

God's standard is His Word. His Word dwells within us and rises up against the enemy. Our faith in and obedience to that Word is our shield, our fortress, our protection.

If you don't know His Word, begin to read it and study it and devour it! If you don't know how to be led by the Holy Spirit, ask Him! He will lead you to the Word which will teach you about yielding to the Spirit. The only way you can be "fed" and then "led" is to feed on God's Word.

"It is written, 'Man shall not live by bread alone, but by every word that proceeds from the mouth of God.'"

Matthew 4:4

The word "proceeds" is present tense, not past tense, meaning it is ongoing. The Spirit has to connect with the Word you have inside of you in order for the Holy Spirit and the Word to agree. How much Word do you have inside you?

"And you shall know the truth, and the truth shall make you free."

John 8:32

God is looking for those who not only know His promises, but who will live by His principles. Then He can fulfill His promises. His Word will set us free!

Manifestations of His Power

When we surrender our ALL to Him and walk in faith, speaking and obeying His Word, then we will begin to see greater manifestations of His Power than we have ever seen before. God is pouring out His Spirit in a greater measure, and He desires that we rise up and enter into what the Spirit of God has come to give us.

Don't wait! Do not fear or pull back. Press your way forward. How? Like the little woman with the issue of blood—with determination! And like Noah—with faith, obedience, and a reverent fear of the Lord, not the fear of men!

Rivers in the Flood

The waves of the rivers of deception, fear, and destruction are now more and more frequent and becoming stronger and stronger. These rivers are real in the natural world, but we must not allow ourselves to focus on them. We must continually remind ourselves that God is greater, and He is still in charge. God has not lost control, nor will He.

Things in the natural world are temporal and subject to change. The only thing which will not change is God's Word. It is truth forever, without even a shadow of turning. It doesn't budge a bit!

"Put Me in remembrance; Let us contend together; State your case, that you may be acquitted."

Isaiah 43:26

God wants us to know our covenant rights and to remind Him of them. We have the right to be healed, the right to be blessed, and the right for our children to walk with the Lord.

Those who choose to enter the Ark and build God's Word

securely around themselves will be sanctified and sealed by His blood and by God's Holy Spirit. They will be brought safely through this last-day flood of the enemy.

"For in Him we live and move and have our being . . ."

Acts 17:28a

Chapter 6

ABRAHAM'S OBEDIENCE

God said to have an "Abraham-kind of faith."

Most people are familiar with the story of Abraham. God told him to leave his country, his father's house and his kinsmen, and travel to a strange faraway land which God would show him.

Why did God want Abraham (then known as Abram) to move and leave everything behind? We learn from Joshua 24:2 that his father, Terah, and other relatives were idolaters. They were moon worshipers living in Ur, a city located on the west bank of the Euphrates River, which was called the "Great River." The Euphrates has since changed its course, so today the ruins of Ur are located in the southern part of Iraq.

God called Abraham out of this idolatrous environment because He had a plan and a purpose for his life. Abraham was a chosen vessel.

"Now the LORD had said to Abram: 'Get out of your country, from your family and from your father's house, to a land that I will show you. I will make you a great nation; I will bless you and make your name great; and you shall be a blessing. I will bless those who bless you, and I will curse him who curses you; and in you all the families of the earth shall be blessed.'"

Genesis 12:1-3

If Abraham would obey and depart from his home where all his kinsmen lived around him and go into a land of uncertainty, a place he would not even know until God revealed it to him, God would then use him to bring forth a great nation.

Fully Persuaded

Abraham was already up in years. He was well-known, comfortable, and used to everything being as it was, so God's instructions probably seemed very strange to him—and most likely seemed insane to his wife, Sarah! But we are told that when God called him, Abraham was fully persuaded. What does it mean to be fully persuaded?

Webster's Dictionary defines "fully" as: "entirely" or "completely." Then "persuade" is defined as "prevailing on a person to do something; induce to believe or convince; influencing someone's thoughts or actions: used mainly in the sense of winning over a person to a certain course of action."

God's voice has been described as sounding like the sound of "many waters." As God of the universe and all creation, He knows how to get a person's attention. Abraham knew he had heard from God! He did not doubt, but believed! He reverently obeyed and fulfilled the Scripture:

"Therefore 'Come out from among them and be separate, says the Lord. Do not touch what is unclean, and I will receive you.'"

2 Corinthians 6:17

Many times he did not understand the "why" of what he was told to do, but faith leaped alive in him and he grabbed hold of what God had spoken. So when God said for him to "go" or "do," he obeyed. Even when he made mistakes—and in the long periods when he did not hear from God at all—Abraham still believed. He believed God had not forgotten and somehow, someway, He would bring it all to pass.

"He who calls you is faithful, who also will do it."

1 Thessalonians 5:24

True faith believes even when nothing seems to be happening. You just know that you know that you know! You believe and see those things as already in existence.

". . . God, who gives life to the dead and calls those things which do not exist as though they did;"

Romans 4:17b

God doesn't change His mind. The gifts and calling of God are irrevocable (Romans 11:29). However, it is our choice whether we believe and answer the call.

Blood Covenant

To cut a blood covenant with another person was the strongest bond one could enter into in the Old Testament. Once a covenant was sealed between the two people, all that each possessed belonged not only to the other, but also to their descendants.

Genesis 15:8-18 tells us that Abraham had entered into a blood covenant with God. God wanted proof that Abraham would be obedient to that covenant. He asked a very hard thing! He asked Abraham to sacrifice his most prized possession, the son he had longed for and waited so many years to receive. God knew if Abraham was willing to surrender his son of promise in total obedience to Him, he would remain faithful to the covenant they had made.

So, one day God called, "Abraham!"

"Here I am," replied Abraham.

"Then He said, 'Take now your son, your only son Isaac, whom you love, and go to the land of Moriah, and offer him there as a burnt offering on one of the mountains of which I shall tell you.'"

Genesis 22:2

God didn't give him a reason why. How did Abraham react? What did he do? The Bible does not record that he tried to determine if he had heard correctly (like we probably would do). He did not ask for a sign or put out a fleece. He did not even try to reason with God or try to get Him to change His mind. He knew God's voice!

But there was also something else Abraham knew. He knew God had promised to make him the father of many nations through Isaac, this son of promise. God was a God of ALL His Word and Abraham knew somehow God would fulfill that covenant promise, regardless of this sacrificial command. Trusting God to be faithful—as He had been in the past—Abraham proceeded to be loyal to the covenant. You will notice, though, he told his servants:

> *"And Abraham said to his young men, 'Stay here with the donkey; the lad and I will go yonder and worship, and we will come back to you.'"*

Genesis 22:5

Also, when Isaac asked about the lamb for the offering, Abraham replied:

> *"And Abraham said, 'My son, God will provide himself a lamb for a burnt offering . . .'"*

Genesis 22:8a (KJV)

He trusted in the One who had caused his barren wife to conceive long after they were both beyond child-bearing age. He didn't know how God would provide, but he believed He would. He was the God of the impossible!

Our Words

> *"For assuredly, I say to you, whoever says to this mountain, 'Be removed and be cast into the sea,' and does not doubt in his*

heart, but believes that those things he says will be done, he will have whatever he says."

Mark 11:23

Abraham was quoting Mark before these words were written. God spoke through Isaiah:

"I create the fruit of the lips . . ."

Isaiah 57:19a

What is coming out of your mouth?

Are you speaking faith and what you desire within God's promises—or doubt and what you fear or dread? What do you believe? Your future, good or bad, is determined by the words you speak.

What does God say?

"Death and life are in the power of the tongue, and those who love it will eat its fruit."

Proverbs 18:21

"For out of the abundance of the heart the mouth speaks. A good man out of the good treasure of his heart brings forth good things, and an evil man out of the evil treasure brings forth evil

things. But I say to you that for every idle word men may speak, they will give account of it in the day of judgment. For by your words you will be justified, and by your words you will be condemned."

Matthew 12:34b-37

Abraham was justified! God not only saw his obedience but also heard words of faith coming out of his mouth. He intervened and provided the lamb for the sacrifice just as Abraham had spoken to Isaac. Can you imagine the rejoicing and praising God that took place on that mountain as he untied and embraced his son?

God's Pledge

God has provided a sacrificial Lamb for us also, along with a brand new covenant. Under the conditions of the new covenant through the blood of Christ Jesus, God has pledged Himself. Indeed, He has bound Himself to us as ONE. It says that we are not only joint-heirs with Abraham and all the promises made to him, but we are also joint-heirs with His Son Jesus (Romans 8:17).

We are one with Jesus, and Jesus is one with the Father. Our new covenant relationship through the shed blood of

Jesus says that all God has belongs to us, and all we have belongs to Him.

Each time we take communion,

we are renewing that covenant

relationship promise with Him.

Hallelujah!

Summary

Abraham knew he had heard from God. He did not know where he was going; but in obedience, he began to move. There were times when he missed it and made mistakes, just like we do. In fact, he messed up badly and had a son who was not of the promise. However, God has said:

"For the gifts and the calling of God are irrevocable."

Romans 11:29

He does not revoke or take back what He gives us.

Abraham did not give up, even though there were long periods when he did not hear from God. He continued to obey God's principles and believe in spite of all odds. In faith, he began to call things that were not as though they already were (Romans 4:17).

Just as God spoke things into being in the beginning, Abraham was speaking, thinking, and believing things before they were visible or tangible. He did not question God's reason or plan, but followed His commands. Also, the Bible does not mention Abraham complaining. He just grabbed hold of what God had spoken and did not let go.

God's Ways are Not Our Ways

We, too, are chosen vessels and are called to leave our idolatrous ways behind us. We are to do and go as God directs, even if we do not understand, and even if it seems unreasonable or far-fetched. He says His ways are not our ways and His thoughts are much higher than our thoughts (Isaiah 55:8-9). We, too, must be fully persuaded that God will fulfill ALL His promises to us.

He has given us His Covenant Word!

Chapter 7

SARAH'S FAITH

What about Sarah? God also said to have the "Sarah-kind of faith."

Sarah believed her husband, Abraham, when he told her that God had promised him an heir. She respected the call God had placed on his life. We are never to envy the call God places on any individual, but to respect, support, and encourage that person.

How Could This Happen?

Sarah had not only been barren and unable to bear children, but she was now way past the reproductive age. Abraham was ten years older than his wife. How could this happen? She believed her husband had heard from God, yet nothing was happening.

How often do we think that sometimes we need to help God out? We think we should do something to help God bring His plan to pass. He doesn't need our help. If He has indeed spoken, then He will see that it takes place—in spite of us. However, our unbelief can hinder Him.

I am sure Sarah and Abraham tried to reason this out by themselves. Maybe Abraham's heir would come through another, instead of Sarah. According to civil laws existing at that time, children of slaves belonged to the master, and such a practice was legal. So Sarah offered her maid, Hagar, to Abraham, and Abraham agreed that maybe this would be the way God would bring about His promise.

An heir did come forth through Hagar, but Sarah soon realized this had been a big mistake. She wanted to correct it, but couldn't. Sometimes we just have to live with the results of our mistakes. As time went by, she probably resigned herself to the fact that this was just the way it was going to be.

But Not God!

The day came when the Lord visited Abraham. Sarah remained in her tent because the women of that day did not eat with male guests (Genesis 18:9). When God inquired about her, she heard her name mentioned and went to the doorway to listen. The tent was behind the men, but she could see the Lord as He talked with her husband.

When God told Abraham the son of promise would yet come forth from Sarah, she couldn't help but laugh at the impossibility of it. She had longed for a son all these years, and now, when it was impossible to happen, God was saying she would bear a child. God heard her, and asked why she laughed. Then Sarah became afraid and denied laughing.

He did not rebuke her, but instead encouraged her.

"Is anything too hard for the LORD? At the appointed time I will return to you, according to the time of life, and Sarah shall have a son."

Genesis 18:14

Gift of Faith

Suddenly, Sarah received the same "gift of faith" to believe Him, just as Abraham had! The "gift of faith" is just that—a gift from God (1 Corinthians 12:9). She did not know how this miracle could be, but now she believed in her heart that somehow it would take place. She knew she had God's Word on it, and now believed that somehow He could do even the impossible.

She joined her faith with Abraham's.

"Again I say to you that if two of you agree on earth concerning anything that they ask, it will be done for them by My Father in heaven."

Matthew 18:19

Sarah's faith and joy in knowing that nothing is too hard for the Lord gave her strength to receive the promise.

". . . for the joy of the Lord is your strength."

Nehemiah 8:10b

Promise Fulfilled

Certainly Sarah was now filled with great joy and anticipation. And God is always true to His Word. He did visit Sarah and she not only received strength to conceive the seed of the promised child, but also carried him to maturity and then delivered him forth. A son was born at the set time of which God had spoken. Glory to God!

God had already spoken in Genesis 17:19 that the child of promise was to be named Isaac, which means "laughter." Sarah's laughter of disbelief turned into faith, then into belief, and then into laughter of joy. She gave God the credit for her laughter and joy.

"And Sarah said, 'God has made me laugh, and all who hear will laugh with me.'"

Genesis 21:6

Be Like Sarah

We need to bind fear and doubt and, like Sarah, begin to laugh at the impossible situations we face and the circumstances we see with the natural eye.

What did God say? We are to trust and believe what God has said about it, and know beyond any doubt that He is well able to perform His promises. He is a performance God!

"And whatever His soul desires, that He does. For He performs what is appointed for me . . ."

Job 23:13b-14a

Is Anything Too Hard for the Lord?

The Word of God has power to transform our failure, lack, and confusion into victory, abundance, and peace each and every day.

God said to Sarah, "Is anything too hard for the Lord?" (Genesis 18:14). Our work is to build up our most holy faith (Jude 20), and joyfully wait for His timing in the matter—however long that takes. We should never murmur nor waver, and certainly never give up.

Summary

Like Sarah, we need to become pregnant with God's Seed, the Word of God. It is up to us to use the measure of faith He has given us, and to get His Word so deep in our spirit that it takes root. And that deeply-rooted Word will develop, grow, mature, and consume us until it cannot be contained any longer, and it brings forth fruit in newness of life—in speech, in actions, and in joy.

We are not to let age or any other seemingly impossible situation discourage us or keep us from serving God. If God can renew the youth of Sarah's productive organs to bring forth a child, He is certainly capable of renewing our productive abilities to bring forth fruit.

Also, He is still able to lead us in ways we have not traveled before, as He did with Abraham, and bring us safely through stormy uncharted waters, as He did for Noah.

True Bible faith believes God's incredible promises, sees the invisible, and receives the impossible!

Chapter 8

GOD'S TIMETABLE

"And we know that we are of God, and the whole world lieth in wickedness."

1 John 5:19 (KJV)

"And saying, Where is the promise of His coming? For since the fathers fell asleep, all things continue as they were from the beginning of creation.'"

2 Peter 3:4 (KJV)

Storm Warning

Thankfully, we are still in the season of His Grace, but all the prophets have warned of a great storm coming in the final days. They said it will beat with fierceness against God's creation. For many years we have heard this warning and at first many listened; but then years passed, and things continued the same.

Instead of a storm, we experienced prosperity. Instead of a crash, we saw a record-breaking boom. America enjoyed great prosperity as she rode a swelling crest of good times. It seemed that the people grew weary of hearing about the great storm that did not come. As the stock market continued to climb and prosper, many in the Church said, "Relax and enjoy the blessings of the Lord." So the gathering clouds in the distance were dismissed as nothing to really worry about.

However, those dark threatening clouds are not distant any-more, and many ungodly rivers are now overflowing. One might ask, "Is the Church today in a famine of hearing? Have we al-ready become the Church of Laodicea saying, 'I am rich and increased with goods and have need of nothing'?" Has the Church, indeed, become lukewarm, blind and dull of hearing (Revelation 3:15-17)?

Christians who are "married" to this world and its "things" will turn off warnings.

Revival

But a real revival fire, a true awakening, is already in progress in America. It is found in small pockets at this time, but is increasing—and God's Word does not return void; it accomplishes what He sends it to do, and prospers in the thing for which He sent it.

"So shall My word be that goes forth from My mouth; it shall not return to Me void, but it shall accomplish what I please, and it shall prosper in the thing for which I sent it. For you shall go out with joy, and be led out with peace; the mountains and the hills shall break forth into singing before you, and all the trees of the field shall clap their hands."

Isaiah 55:11-12

Our country is now in a position to move toward God. God is still in control; and when He moves things can change quickly, even drastically.

"For there are three that bear witness in heaven: the Father, the Word, and the Holy Spirit; and these three are one. And there are three that bear witness on earth: the Spirit, the water, and the blood; and these three agree as one. If we receive the witness of men, the witness of God is greater; for this is the witness of God which He has testified of His Son . . . We know that whoever is born of God does not sin; but he who has been born of God keeps himself, and the wicked one does not touch him."

1 John 5:7-9, 18

We have scriptural proof that God will reveal His glory and miraculously carry His true Believers through all the calamities which could happen. Yes, He will provide, even supernaturally if necessary, if we are seeking and trusting Him with all of our heart.

He says to seek Him early while He can be found, not after the storm hits. Remember Elijah's experience in 1 Kings 19:11-12. The Lord was not in the strong wind which destroyed the mountains and broke rocks in pieces. He was not in the earthquake. He was not in the fire. God came in a still, small voice.

It is easy to have faith when the sun is shining and all is going well. But where is our faith when the storm clouds have gathered and things are beginning to look darker and darker?

Faith is the substance of things hoped for, and Jesus is the hope of our glory. That is what our faith is all about: knowing that Jesus has already paid the price for our salvation, our healing, our protection, our provision, and our prosperity. He has paid the price for our very life!

He is the "Way." The Way not only for life eternal, but the Way through all the problems and difficulties of each and every day of this earthly life. So keep praising God, for the Bible says in Romans 8:31b:

". . . If God be for us, who can be against us?"

Chapter 9

OUR PASSOVER PROMISE

When God delivered the children of Israel out of bondage to the Egyptians, the blood of an ordinary lamb was enough to ensure the safety of an entire household. It took only one person applying the blood of the sacrificial lamb to stand between life and death for the whole house.

Are you that person today?

God's Prophetic Passover Promise

"And the blood shall be to you for a token upon the houses where ye are: and when I see the blood, I will pass over you, and the plague shall not be upon you to destroy you . . ."

Exodus 12:13 (KJV)

Our own deliverance from the enemy's bondage and eternal death was birthed in that original Passover.

Life itself is spiritual, but it must have a physical carrier, and this carrier is the blood. Blood does not control the color of the skin or the culture of the person; it simply carries the life which comes from God.

"For the life of the flesh is in the blood, and I have given it to you upon the altar to make atonement for your souls; for it is the blood that makes atonement for the soul."

Leviticus 17:11

Sacrificial Blood

Today, the blood of the Pure Lamb, Christ Jesus, which was shed on the altar of Calvary, makes atonement for all who will receive it.

So we, through prayer in the name of Jesus—that name which is above every name named—can apply that sacrificial blood. We can spiritually place His blood on the doorpost of our home, and also the homes of our children.

By doing so, we come under that prophetic Passover promise. We can then demand and claim in the name of Jesus that Satan's hold on all of our loved ones is broken and he has to pass on by. We place them under the heritage of the Creator Father. It is our God-given right to expect salvation for our entire household.

"For I will pour water on him who is thirsty, and floods on the dry ground; I will pour My Spirit on your descendants, and My blessing on your offspring"

Isaiah 44:3

"For the promise is to you and to your children, and to all who are afar off, as many as the Lord our God will call."

Acts 2:39

The blood of Jesus is the basis for our salvation. Then our part is not only to accept that truth, but also add our testimony and confession to it.

"And they overcame him by the blood of the Lamb and by the word of their testimony, and they did not love their lives to the death."

Revelation 12:11

We Have Been Given Authority

W e need to use the authority He has given us and start speaking our promises into existence.

". . . God, who gives life to the dead and calls those things which do not exist as though they did."

Romans 4:17b

Claim every promise God has given. Search out the scripture which gives the promise you desire and need. Remind God of it. He already knows His promises because He wrote them; however, He wants us to know them as well and use our faith to receive them. The Bible says without faith it is impossible to please Him (Hebrews 11:6).

Maybe some "wrong" things have taken place, but God always has a scripture, a wonderful promise which will cover the situation. Also, we must always seek God's will, not our will. He knows the end from the beginning and what is best for us. He is for us, not against us and is well able to turn any situation around and bring good out of it (Romans 8:28).

As we walk in God's commandments and principles, He

will shod our feet with iron and bronze. We can walk our days in His power and His strength.

> *"Your sandals shall be iron and bronze; as your days, so shall your strength be."*

Deuteronomy 33:25

Chapter 10

BUILDING THE ARK

We receive eternal life by believing, accepting, and confessing Jesus Christ as our Savior. But to live victoriously as an overcomer, we need to also make Him Lord of our life, be Holy Spirit filled and Spirit led.

How Do We Build Our Ark?

How do we build an Ark to save our households? If you believe the Word, you have a foundation to build upon. God said to build it with His Word and our obedience. Settle on the fact that His Word is true and it is forever. It does not change. He said the world will pass away, but His Word will never pass away.

We must become willing to line ourselves up with His Word. It is our lifeline. We must separate ourselves from the cares and worries of the world and spend time with Him.

Be a Doer of the Word

1. DO EVERYTHING IN LOVE

First of all, we build it with love. Remember, the Word says: "Now abideth faith, hope and love; but the greatest of these is love," (1 Corinthians 13:13). We are to do everything in love, and not think more highly of ourselves than we ought. (Study 1 Corinthians 13.)

Have you heard the expression: "walk softly and carry a big stick"? To me, that is to walk in love with the power of the Holy Spirit. God is all-power, and you can't have a bigger stick than that!

2. APPLY HIS PROMISES

To "build" is "to apply." God wants us to not only obey His commandments, but to claim and apply His promises to each and every need. His life is in each promise; and as we walk in that promise, it comes alive for us. "If we live in the Spirit, let us also walk in the Spirit" (Galatians 5:25).

Every promise in God's Word has been paid for. His promises are "life stones" dipped in the sacrificial blood of

Jesus, with Jesus being the Chief Cornerstone. These stones, these promises, are full of the life of God. Through faith, we take hold of each one and build these promises in and around our lives. We become as "living stones" building up a spiritual house, a holy priesthood, acceptable to God (1 Peter 2:5).

God knows our needs, but He is moved by our faith. *"But without faith it is impossible to please Him . . ."* (Hebrews 11:6). As we apply His promises to our needs, they begin to work on our behalf. The Word will work—if we work the Word!

3. REALIZE YOU ARE NEVER ALONE.

He does not leave us to build alone.

> *"For He Himself has said, 'I will never leave you nor forsake you.' So we may boldly say: 'The LORD is my helper; I will not fear. What can man do to me?'"*

Hebrews 13:5b-6

He promises us His strength, and we can be confident that He will help us to follow His directions throughout life. But it takes our faith and commitment.

"I can do all things through Christ who strengthens me."

Philippians 4:13

"Being confident of this, that he who began a good work in you will carry it on to completion until the day of Christ Jesus."

Philippians 1:6 (NIV)

4. BELIEVE

God is Spirit, so His Word is also Spirit. It is spiritual and it is truth; it will never change. You can stake your very life on it.

If what we see around us with our natural eye does not line up with what God says about it, then it is subject to change. Through our faith and obedience, His Word—that Spiritual Ark—will rise above every need, every sickness, and every lack. It will cover and fulfill all that we need.

5. SEEK

He said for us to seek Him early while He can be found (Isaiah55:6a). That not only means early in the morning before we get caught up in the cares and business of the day, but early in each problem or situation which comes up. If we ask for His advice, His help, and His guidance in the matter before we try to handle it ourselves, we can usually save ourselves a lot of worry, heartache, and disappointment.

God can turn our problems around for our good instead of to our harm. There is no better problem solver than God. He may work it out completely different than we had anticipated. Most of the time, the solution will be a lot better than we had ever hoped for. God is an amazing God!

"Every good gift and every perfect gift is from above, and comes down from the Father of lights, with whom there is no variation or shadow of turning."

James 1:17

6. ACT

We must act upon His Word. Study it. Meditate upon it. Find scriptures that cover the situation. Then, put the Word to work.   It will pass every test! Speak it! Claim it! Use it! Stand on it! Surround everyone and everything with it. We are told to have His Word constantly in our heart and in our mouth. He said to simply trust Him as a little child would trust.

7. PRAY

"But the end of all things is at hand; therefore be serious and watchful in your prayers."

1 Peter 4:7

Prayer is simply talking to God like we talk to our best friend. In fact, He is our best friend! He already knows our needs and our hearts, but He wants us to turn to Him in faith. When we discuss things with Him, He can begin to change the situation.

Today, the family is under more pressure to break apart than any other time in our history. Our children are prime targets for satanic attacks. We need to zero in on the salvation and protection of every member of our household.

First, check yourself. Make sure you are clean before the Lord. Repent of anything and everything that would not be pleasing to Him. Repentance is essential, for Jesus said:

". . . unless you repent you will all likewise perish."

Luke 13:3

To repent is not just to say you are sorry, but you must completely turn away from it. Without repentance, there is no salvation. Acts 17:30-31a tells us:

"Truly, these times of ignorance God overlooked, but now commands all men everywhere to repent, because He has appointed a day on which He will judge the world in righteousness by the Man (Jesus) whom He has ordained."

Cover yourself and your loved ones daily with the blood of Jesus. Put on the whole armor of God. (Study Ephesians 6:10-18.) For our battle is not with flesh and blood, but with the wiles of the devil. Satan is our real enemy; and he will use not only problems and circumstances to come against us, but also unsuspecting people.

Check to see if you might be holding a grudge or if you have any unforgiveness in your heart. You must get rid of it. Forgive them and even ask God to bless them. You may not mean it from your heart, but ask God to help you mean it.

8. PERSONALIZE YOUR RELATIONSHIP WITH GOD

God is a personal God. He loves each one individually, so call your name when quoting His promises. Make them personal. Put your name or your loved one's name in there.

Ask the Holy Spirit to teach you. Ask Him to instruct and show you the way to go. Ask Him to go before you and prepare the way and keep you on the right path. If you stay Scripture-based, you'll be Scripture-led and full of joy!

> *"I will instruct you and teach you in the way you should go; I will guide you with My eye. Do not be like the horse or like the mule, which have no understanding, which must be harnessed with bit and bridle, else they will not come near you. Many sorrows shall be to the wicked; but he who trusts in the LORD, mercy shall surround him. Be glad in the LORD and rejoice, you righteous; and shout for joy, all you upright in heart!"*

Psalms 32:8-11

9. USE YOUR AUTHORITY

Are your children running around with the wrong crowd; those who belong to the enemy? Do warfare! As Believers, we have the authority of Jesus. He gave it to those who believe in Him. That means you and me!

> *"And I will give you the keys of the kingdom of heaven, and whatever you bind on earth will be bound in heaven, and whatever you loose on earth will be loosed in heaven."*

Matthew 16:19

After covering yourself and your loved ones with the blood of Jesus, begin to bind those wrong friends out of their lives and loose Godly friends to replace them. Ask God to station angels around them with their flaming swords to ward off the fiery darts of the devil.

Pull down every stronghold which Satan has built up in anyone, and put those strongholds under your feet and under the feet of Jesus. Then stomp all over them and call them "null and void."

10. BE SPECIFIC

Call each one of your loved ones by name and give them to the Lord. Continue to stand in the gap "calling those things that be not as though they were," (Romans 4:17b).

Faith and obedience will remove mountains— mountains of evil, mountains of fear and difficulty—but faith and obedience must go hand in hand. If you believe with your heart, say with your mouth, and do not doubt that it will come to pass, you will have what you say (Mark 11:23-24). Use your faith and your voice. Speak to that mountain of lack and to that mountain which has your children bound. Command it to move and be gone in the almighty powerful name of Jesus!

Remember that "unbelief " believes only what it sees, but "faith" sees what it believes! In your spirit, see each one as saved, healed, delivered, walking close to God, and with a good job, out of debt, and prosperous—or whatever is needed!

Picture them as the finished product.

Don't give up! Keep praising God for victory, even when you can't see any changes. If you are praying God's Word over the situation, then you are praying according to His Will.

> *"Now this is the confidence that we have in Him, that if we ask anything according to His will, He hears us. And if we know that He hears us, whatever we ask, we know that we have the petitions that we have asked of Him."*

1 John 5:14-15

If you have a prayer partner who believes like you do, you might want to ask them to join you in the prayer of agreement.

"Again I say to you that if two of you agree on earth concerning anything that they ask, it will be done for them by My Father in heaven. For where two or three are gathered together in My name, I am there in the midst of them."

Matthew 18:19-20

Faith-filled Words Have Great Power

The key to faith is to believe it and say it before it is manifested! Put your faith into action with the words of your mouth!

"Thus also faith by itself, if it does not have works, is dead."

James 2:17

Start speaking God's promise for what you are believing. Start calling those things that are not as though they already are. Just thinking them with your mind won't work. You must believe in your heart that God's promise is the way things should be, then talk it—speak it out.

Even God had to "speak" what He wanted when He said, "Let there be light." He could have just talked with the angels about how dark everything was. Instead, He spoke the end result into existence. He has given us this same authority through the name of Jesus when we make Jesus our Lord and Savior.

At first, this may seem like you are not speaking the truth, but God's Word is Truth; and when we line our thoughts and words up with His Word, then our temporal situation can be changed.

Speak His Word!

Chapter 11

STAY FOCUSED

"And let us not grow weary while doing good, for in due season we shall reap if we do not lose heart."

Galatians 6:9

When you take a stand to believe God, the enemy will send challenges. He will throw up roadblocks and distractions to knock you off course. But you will be amazed at what God will do when you stand firm and face your challenges and hold on to the promises in His Word. Take a stand in your prayer life. Take a stand in your Bible study time. Take a stand in serving and giving to others.

Take a stand and see the salvation and provision of the Lord!

"Do not be afraid. Stand still, and see the salvation of the LORD, which He will accomplish for you today."

Exodus 14:13

Just as Noah obeyed and pushed ahead to do all that God called him to do, we also must push ahead in spite of obstacles and hindrances. We must remain faithful, obedient, and focused. We must keep at it and keep building that Ark no matter how long it takes. Remember, these are precious souls for eternity. Someday they will rise up and call you "blessed" (Proverbs 31:28).

God Will Personally Seal Our Ark

God personally sealed Noah's Ark for the safety of Noah and his household during the Great Flood in that day. He will do the same for us today.

There is no security outside the Ark that God offers. The world cannot give it to us, and we cannot attain it on our own. But the very day we get serious with Jesus and His promises, our divine protection begins. We may see havoc in the world around us, but God is able to carry us safely through all the tributaries feeding the enemy's flood. They cannot overflow us.

When I study the Bible and see all that is coming upon the earth because of Man's wickedness, I weep in gratitude for God's protective Ark. I weep for joy that we belong to Him and that He takes care of His own.

Delay Can be Deadly

We find, however, in the book of Haggai that God told the people they had procrastinated. They had delayed working on God's house, saying it was not time for that. Instead of doing God's work, they were busy working on their own personal affairs. Their time, efforts, and money were spent on their own matters and interests—and little or none on the Lord's.

God told them to consider their ways. There was no lasting peace or joy. They worked hard, but it was like they were putting their wages in a bag with holes in it. There never seemed to be enough; they needed and wanted more and more.

God is again saying, "Consider your ways." He says to be strong and build the house of the Lord, and He will take pleasure in it.

Where is Our Seed?

"Is the seed still in the barn? As yet the vine, the fig tree, the pomegranate, and the olive tree have not yielded fruit. But from this day I will bless you."

Haggai 2:19

Why are our children, grandchildren, and others we love and care about still in bondage to this world? Why have they not been set free?

We can set them free to enter into the Ark through prayers and intercession. Remember, God is looking for those who will live by His principles—His instructions—so He can give them His promises.

We must keep the Word of God coming into our hearts by hearing it and studying it, then letting it come back out through our mouths until it overflows in our lives. It has power not only to transform our lives but also the lives of those we are praying for. It can change failure, lack, and confusion into victory and bring abundance, joy, and peace.

We must work the work of God before it is too late. Even if we can't see any results in the natural, like Abraham and Sarah, we know that we know in our heart that God is at work.

From the day we begin to build, God said He will bless us.

Victory in Praise!

"Enter into His gates with thanksgiving, and into His courts with praise. Be thankful to Him, and bless His name."

Psalms 100:4

We thank Him and praise Him for His promises both before and after they are fulfilled.

If it sounds like I keep repeating and repeating myself—yes, I am! We are in the end of the end times. Time is short, and lives are at stake. We must work the works of God while it is still day because the time is fast approaching when no man can work (John 9:4).

If we keep looking unto Jesus, His eternal life is ours.

Doubt flees, joy reigns,
and hope conquers.

Chapter 12

GOOD NEWS!
ANOTHER RIVER IS FLOWING!

"And he shewed me a pure river of water of life, clear as crystal, proceeding out of the throne of God and of the Lamb."

Revelation 22:1

Today, there is wonderful news! Even though satanic rivers are flooding the world, there is another river flowing—not a river of darkness, but a river of Light.

A River of Life

There is life in this river and glorious revival fires are igniting. God said in the last days He would pour out His Spirit on all flesh (Joel 2:28, Acts 2:17). It is breaking now upon all who will say, "God, here am I. Send me!" Signs, wonders, and miracles of God will follow those who believe!

I believe the last great harvest of souls has begun, and no flood of this world can overflow the River of Life which flows from the Throne of God. What an exciting and awesome day this is!

Word from the Lord

The day God has prepared us for is upon us. A well-known international prophet/evangelist has prophesied:

> *"For thus saith the Lord, every vision shall escalate. That which took years to accomplish in the past shall be fulfilled in a matter of months. I have told you to prepare for this day. Now it is upon you.*
>
> *If you cannot go with the footmen, and the horsemen have wearied you, what will be your portion in this day? Press on toward your mark, faint not. The harvest is upon you. Let not any of the precious grain fall to waste, for it is precious indeed.*
>
> *Hear the voice of the Spirit. You have much to do. Labor not in vain with the things of this world, for they are only temporal. Put your energies into the things that are eternal. Then shall your reward be great."*

Praise God for the voice of the Spirit which is going forth in the earth. Time is short. What we do for God must be done now. This is not doom and gloom, but joy unspeakable that our Lord is returning soon.

The end of all flesh is again coming before God, for the earth is as it was in the days of Noah. The wickedness of Man is great and the imaginations and thoughts of his heart are continually filled with evil and violence (Genesis 6:5).

Dark Days Ahead

To those outside the protection of God's Ark, the days ahead will be alarming. The scoffers in the land will continue to walk after their own lusts. The Bible says they do not fear God and are willingly ignorant.

"And saying, 'Where is the promise of His coming? For since the fathers fell asleep, all things continue as they were from the beginning of creation.' For this they willfully forget: that by the word of God the heavens were of old, and the earth standing out of water and in the water, by which the world that then existed perished, being flooded with water. But the heavens and the earth which are now preserved by the same word, are reserved for fire until the day of judgment and perdition of ungodly men."

2 Peter 3:4-7

Just as the people ignored God's warnings in Noah's day, many continue to disregard God's warnings in this day. By doing so, they have opened themselves to a flood of all manner of deception, false teaching, and wrong information. They could become like the disobedient servant in Matthew 24 who doubted Jesus' return and ended up acting like the world. The Lord said the day of His return will be unexpected, and disobedient servants will then be appointed the same portion as the hypocrites.

"But if that evil servant says in his heart, 'My master is delaying his coming,' and begins to beat his fellow servants, and to eat and drink with the drunkards, the master of that servant will come on a day when he is not looking for him and at an hour that he is not aware of, and will cut him in two and appoint him his portion with the hypocrites. There shall be weeping and gnashing of teeth."

Matthew 24:48-51

Suddenly! It could happen suddenly—and maybe even sooner than we think. God says "Woe" to those who are deceived or remain asleep.

Do Not Fear

But praise God, we are not asleep and our safety does not rest in the knowledge of men or the things of this world.

We don't need to fear the darkness; because if we set our love and trust on the Lord God, He is always there for us.

"Because he has set his love upon Me, therefore I will deliver him; I will set him on high, because he has known My name. He shall call upon Me, and I will answer him; I will be with him in trouble; I will deliver him and honor him. With long life I will satisfy him, and show him My salvation."

Psalm 91:14-16

Chapter 13

WE ARE CHOSEN

"For many are called, but few are chosen."

Matthew 22:14

Many are called. The fact is that God does not want any to be lost. But, as He knows all things, He already knows who will respond and who will not.

It is up to us to respond and receive the rain of the Holy Spirit that is breaking upon us now. So you see, it is really our choice to be one of His "chosen."

To be chosen by God is the highest calling one can receive. Your current task may not seem very important, but He sees the end from the beginning. He works all things, not only for our good, but for His plan and His purpose (Romans 8:28).

As His chosen, it is important that we build up our most holy faith; where we can believe for what is invisible and receive the impossible! It is all in His Word.

What an awesome way to live!

God said to build an Ark for the saving of our household. It must be built before the storm hits and carries some of our loved ones away.

"Who then is a faithful and wise servant, whom his master made ruler over his household, to give them food in due season? Blessed is that servant whom his master, when he comes, will find so doing. Assuredly, I say to you that he will make him ruler over all his goods."

Matthew 24:45-47

God's Timing

We can claim victory in every situation we face, as there is nothing left uncovered in God's Word. He is the answer. He is the way. He has made provision for any and every circumstance, but the timing is up to Him. Remember,

Noah and Abraham both had a sovereign "word from God," but they had to wait on His timing for that word to come to pass . . . And so do we!

Some scriptures have been listed in the back of this book to help us get started in building an Ark for our loved ones, our protection, and our needs. The Bible is full of many others. Search them out. God is faithful, but we must pray in accordance (in agreement) with His Word.

He will do nothing if it does not agree with the promise He has already provided in His covenant Word.

God is a Performance God

As we believe and continue to speak the Word in spite of the trials and tests which come against us, we have His promise of victory. God watches over His Word to perform it. He is a performance God! In His perfect timing we will see the hand of the Almighty move on our behalf.

His Covenant Word!

"'As for Me,' says the LORD, 'this is My covenant with them: My Spirit who is upon you, and My words which I have put in your mouth, shall not depart from your mouth, nor from the

mouth of your descendants, nor from the mouth of your descendants' descendants,' says the LORD, 'from this time and forevermore.'"

Isaiah 59:21

Our faith declares that all in our household and all of our loved ones are not only saved through Christ Jesus but are also solidly enclosed in the safety of God's living Ark. No flood from the enemy can overflow any of us.

Chapter 14

CONCLUSION

God Said to have "the Noah-kind" of Faith

G od's Word, His Covenant Ark, is our appointed place and our haven from the enemy's flood of today. We are not only to believe, but stay focused and put our faith into action. We build and secure our Ark by speaking God's Word, instead of speaking the problems we face.

We will not doubt or fear, but will stand firm and obedient in spite of the demonic rivers coming against us. Through faith, our household is sealed in, protected and provided for.

...And "the Abraham-kind" of Faith

W e are to be sensitive to the voice of God and the leading of the Holy Spirit. We are to "do" and "go" as God directs. In faith, we speak what God says instead of what we see in the natural, which needs to be changed.

Even if we miss it at times and fail, we get back up. We grab hold of what God has promised and do not let go. Regardless of how long it takes, we are fully persuaded that God will fulfill all He has spoken.

...Also, "the Sarah-kind" of Faith

No matter what our age or situation, we are to become pregnant with God's Seed, which is His Word. Through faith, that Word will take root, grow, and mature within us so we can birth it and bring it forth not only for our good, but also to bless others.

His love and joy cannot be contained, but will burst forth for all to see. We are to be His witnesses in all the earth.

...What About God's Faith?

Had you thought about the faith of God Himself? That He had to have so much faith in us—faith that we would turn from our wicked ways and seek Him—that

He was willing to send His only beloved Son, Jesus, to die for us?

> *"In the beginning was the Word, and the Word was with God, and the Word was God. The Word became flesh and dwelt among us and we beheld His glory, the glory as of the only begotten of the Father, full of grace and truth."*

John 1:1,14

With the shedding of His atoning blood, burial and resurrection, Jesus, the Word of God, has provided us with His Covenant Ark. It is our only place of safety in the midst of a corrupt and evil world.

So, are we a wise servant continuing to pray, intercede, believe, stand on God's promises, speak the Word, and call those things that be not as though they are? Are we plugging every hole? Are we sealing every crack?

Don't wait! Start building your covenant Ark with God now. No storm, no flood, no situation is too difficult for Him.

Remember, eternal life is forever!

Where is your vision?

Where is your faith?

JESUS IS COMING SOON!

Prayer

Dear Father God,

We desire Your eternal Ark to be so strong and sturdy in our lives that we cannot be moved or shaken.

We place the blood of Jesus anew and afresh over ourselves and over all of our loved ones. We apply the oil of the Holy Spirit which empowers us, and we boldly declare God's promises are ours.

We claim our faith is strong, and we stagger not at the promises of God through unbelief.

Like Abraham, we declare ourselves to be fully persuaded that what You have promised, You are well able to perform.

May we become pregnant with the Seed of Your Word. We are believing for that Word to grow within us and become so strong that it will bring forth precious fruit for the glory of God.

We declare that no flood shall overflow us, that no weapon formed against us shall prosper, and that when we go through fire it shall not be kindled against us.

We call those things that are not as though they are. Like Sarah, we laugh at the impossible. Our faith knows that nothing is too hard for the Lord. You can change the impossible to be possible.

Our Ark, like Noah's, rises above the flood of the enemy. It rides in victory for every salvation, every health problem, our finances and every financial decision, every need or lack, every job complication, every relationship, and any situation which touches our lives, whether big or small.

We ask you, Father God, to guide every decision made so it will be for our good. And let our words and actions bring glory to our Lord Jesus.

In His name we pray.

Amen.

Salvation

"*Believe on the Lord Jesus Christ, and thou shalt be saved, and thy house.*"

Acts 16:31b (KJV)

If you have not received Jesus as your Savior, and you want to be included in the protection of His Spiritual Ark, pray this prayer:

Jesus, I ask You to come into my heart and be Lord of my life. I'm sorry for my sins; please forgive me. I believe You are the Son of God; that You were born of a virgin, died for my sins, rose again from the dead, and are now seated with God, the Father, in Heaven. I ask You to fill me with Your Holy Spirit that I may live for you.

Thank You that I am now a new creature in Christ Jesus and a child of God. I believe and receive Your Word in 1 John 4:4 which says:

"You are of God, little children, and have overcome them, because He who is in you is greater than he who is in the world."

Thank you, Father. In Jesus' name. Amen.

Promise Scriptures

These scriptures are not listed in any particular order. If you don't find one here covering your situation, search the Bible. It is filled with His wonderful promises to cover every need.

Blessings:

"And let us not be weary in well doing: for in due season we shall reap, if we faint not."

Galatians 6:9 (KJV)

"I have been young, and now am old; yet have I not seen the righteous forsaken, nor his seed begging bread. He is ever merciful, and lendeth; and his seed is blessed."

Psalms 37:25-26 (KJV)

"For I know the thoughts that I think toward you, saith the Lord, thoughts of peace, and not of evil, to give you an expected end. . . . And ye shall seek me, and find me, when ye shall search for me with all your heart."

Jeremiah 29:11, 13 (KJV)

"And the Lord said, Who then is that faithful and wise steward, whom his lord shall make ruler over his household, to give them their portion of meat in due season? Blessed is that servant, whom his lord when He cometh shall find so doing. Of a truth I say unto you, that he will make him ruler over all that he hath."

Luke 12:42-44 (KJV)

"He will bless them that fear the Lord, both small and great. The Lord shall increase you more and more, you and your children."

Psalms 115:13-14 (KJV)

"Give, and it shall be given unto you; good measure, pressed down, and shaken together, and running over, shall men give

into your bosom. For with the same measure that ye mete withal (give or do for others) it shall be measured to you again."

Luke 6:38 (KJV)

"But my God shall supply all your need according to his riches in glory by Christ Jesus."

Philippians 4:19 (KJV)

"For I will pour water upon him that is thirsty, and floods upon the dry ground: I will pour my spirit upon thy seed, and my blessing upon thine offspring."

Isaiah 44:3 (KJV)

"Now it shall come to pass, if you diligently obey the voice of the LORD your God, to observe carefully all His commandments which I command you today, that the LORD your God will set you high above all nations of the earth. And all these blessings shall come upon you and overtake you, because you obey the voice of the LORD your God: Blessed shall you be in the city, and blessed shall you be in the country. Blessed shall be the fruit of your body, the produce of your ground and the increase of your herds, the increase of your cattle and the offspring of your flocks.

Blessed shall be your basket and your kneading bowl. Blessed shall you be when you come in, and blessed shall you be when you go out. The LORD will cause your enemies who rise against you to be defeated before your face; they shall come out against you one way and flee before you seven ways.

The LORD will command the blessing on you in your storehouses and in all to which you set your hand, and He will bless you in the land which the LORD your God is giving you. The LORD will establish you as a holy people to Himself, just as He has sworn to you, if you keep the commandments of the LORD your God and walk in His ways. Then all peoples of the earth shall see that you are called by the name of the LORD, and they shall be afraid of you. And the LORD will grant you plenty of goods, in the fruit of your body, in the increase of your livestock, and in the produce of your ground, in the land of which the LORD swore to your fathers to give you.

The LORD will open to you His good treasure, the heavens, to give the rain to your land in its season, and to bless all the work of your hand. You shall lend to many nations, but you shall not borrow. And the LORD will make you the head and not the tail; you shall be above only, and not be beneath, if you heed the commandments of the LORD your God, which I command you today, and are careful to observe them. So you shall not turn aside from any of the words which I command you this day, to the right or the left, to go after other gods to serve them."

Deuteronomy 28:1-14

"So shall my word be that goeth forth out of my mouth: it shall not return unto me void, but it shall accomplish that which I please, and it shall prosper in the thing whereto I sent it."

Isaiah 55:11 (KJV)

Boldness:

". . . grant unto thy servants, that with all boldness, they may speak thy word, by stretching forth thine hand to heal; and that signs and wonders may be done by the name of thy holy child Jesus."

Acts 4:29b-30 (KJV)

Comforter:

"But the Comforter, which is the Holy Ghost, whom the Father will send in my name, he shall teach you all things, and bring all things to your remembrance, whatsoever I have said unto you."

John 14:26 (KJV)

Eternal Life:

"And I give unto them eternal life; and they shall never perish, neither shall any man pluck them out of my hand."

John 10:28 (KJV)

Faith:

". . . even God, who quickeneth the dead, and calleth those things which be not as though they were."

Romans 4:17b (KJV)

"Ye have not chosen me, but I have chosen you, and ordained you, that ye should go and bring forth fruit, and that your fruit should remain: that whatsoever ye shall ask of the Father in my name, he may give it you."

John 15:16 (KJV)

"Have faith in God. For verily I say unto you, That whosoever shall say unto this mountain, Be thou removed, and be thou cast *into the sea; and shall not doubt in his heart, but shall believe that those things which he saith shall come to pass; he shall have whatsoever he saith. Therefore I say unto you, What things soever ye desire, when ye pray, believe that ye receive them, and ye shall have them."*

Mark 11:22b-24 (KJV)

Forgive:

"And when ye stand praying, forgive, if ye have ought against any: that your Father also, which is in heaven may forgive you your trespasses. But if ye do not forgive, neither will your Father which is in heaven forgive your trespasses."

Mark 11: 25-26 (KJV)

Forgiveness:

"And the prayer of faith shall save the sick, and the Lord shall raise him up; and if he have committed sins, they shall be forgiven him."

James 5:15 (KJV)

Fruit:

"Those that be planted in the house of the Lord shall flourish in the courts of our God. They shall still bring forth fruit in old age; they shall be fat and flourishing (strong and healthy); To shew that the Lord is upright . . ."

Psalms 92:13-15a (KJV)

Family:

"Lift up thine eyes round about, and see: all they gather themselves together, they come to thee: thy sons shall come from far, and thy daughters shall be nursed at thy side. Then thou shalt see, and flow together, and thine heart shall fear, and be enlarged . . ."

Isaiah 60:4-5a (KJV)

"For the promise is unto you, and to your children, and to all that are afar off, even as many as the Lord our God shall call."

Acts 2:39 (KJV)

"Let thy work appear unto thy servants, and thy glory unto their children."

Psalms 90:16 (KJV)

"That our sons may be as plants grown up in their youth: that our daughters may be as corner stones, polished after the similitude of a palace: That our garners may be full, affording all manner of store . . ."

Psalms 144:12-13a (KJV)

Guidance:

"And I will give unto thee the keys of the kingdom of heaven: and whatsoever thou shalt bind on earth shall be bound in heaven: and whatsoever thou shalt loose on earth shall be loosed in heaven."

Matthew 16:19 (KJV)

"I will instruct thee and teach thee in the way which thou shalt go: I will guide thee with mine eye."

Psalms 32:8 (KJV)

"Ye shall not afflict any widow, or fatherless child. If thou afflict them in any wise, and they cry at all unto me, I will surely hear their cry; and my wrath shall wax hot, and I will kill you with the sword; and your wives shall be widows, and your children fatherless."

Exodus 22:22-24 (KJV)

"If ye be willing and obedient, ye shall eat the good of the land."

Isaiah 1:19 (KJV)

"Let your conversation be without covetousness (envy); and be content with such things as ye have: for he hath said, I will never leave thee, nor forsake thee. So that we may boldly say, The Lord is my helper, and I will not fear what man shall do unto me."

Hebrews 13:5-6 (KJV)

"Therefore all things whatsoever ye would that men should do to you, do ye even so to them: for this is the law and the prophets."

Matthew 7:12 (KJV)

Healing:

"Bless the Lord, O my soul, and forget not all his benefits: who forgiveth all thine iniquities; who healeth all thy diseases; who redeemeth thy life from destruction; who crowneth thee with loving-kindness and tender mercies; who satisfieth thy mouth with good things; so that thy youth is renewed like the eagle's."

Psalms 103:2-5 (KJV)

"And if the Spirit of him who raised Jesus from the dead is living in you, he who raised Christ from the dead will also give life to your mortal bodies through his Spirit, who lives in you."

Romans 8:11 (NIV)

"And the Lord will take away from thee all sickness, and will put none of the evil diseases of Egypt, which thou knowest, upon thee . . ."

Deuteronomy 7:15a (KJV)

"Who (Jesus) his own self bare our sins in his own body on the tree, that we, being dead to sins, should live unto righteousness: by whose stripes ye were healed."

1 Peter 2:24 (KJV)

"And ye shall serve the Lord your God, and he shall bless thy bread, and thy water; and I will take sickness away from the midst of thee. There shall nothing cast their young, nor be barren, in thy land: the number of thy days I will fulfill."

Exodus 23:25-26 (KJV)

"He sent his word, and healed them, and delivered them from their destructions."

Psalm 107:20

His Presence:

"Again I say unto you, That if two of you shall agree on earth as touching any thing that they shall ask, it shall be done for them of my Father which is in heaven. For where two or three are gathered together in my name, there am I in the midst of them."

Matthew 18:19-20 (KJV)

Holy Ghost:

"But ye shall receive power, after that the Holy Ghost is come upon you: and ye shall be witnesses unto me both in Jerusalem, and in all Judea, and in Samaria, and unto the uttermost part of the earth."

Acts 1:8 (KJV)

Hope:

". . . God is no respecter of persons: but in every nation he that feareth him, and worketh righteousness, is accepted with him."

Acts 10:34b-35 (KJV)

"And he said, The things which are impossible with men are possible with God."

Luke 18:27 (KJV)

"And we know that all things work together for good to them that love God, to them who are the called according to his purpose."

Romans 8:28 (KJV)

"Thus saith the Lord; Refrain thy voice from weeping, and thine eyes from tears: for thy work shall be rewarded, saith the Lord; and they shall come again from the land of the enemy. And there is hope in thine end, saith the Lord, that thy children shall come again to their own border."

Jeremiah 31:16-17 (KJV)

"I can do all things through Christ which strengtheneth me."

Philippians 4:13 (KJV)

"Fear not: for I am with thee: I will bring thy seed from the east, and gather thee from the west; I will say to the north, Give up; and to the south, Keep not back: bring my sons from far, and my daughters from the ends of the earth; Even every one that is called by my name: for I have created him for my glory . . ."

Isaiah 43:5-7a (KJV)

"Being confident of this very thing, that he which hath begun a good work in you will perform (or complete) it until the day of Jesus Christ."

Philippians 1:6 (KJV)

"For with God nothing shall be impossible."

Luke 1:37 (KJV)

"Write the vision, and make it plain upon tables, that he may run that readeth it. For the vision is yet for an appointed time, but at the end it shall speak, and not lie: though it tarry, wait for it; because it will surely come, it will not tarry."

Habakkuk 2:2b-3 (KJV)

Indwelling of His Spirit:

"For we are laborers together with God: ye are God's husbandry, ye are God's building . . . But let every man take heed how he buildeth thereupon . . . Know ye not that ye are the temple of God, and that the Spirit of God dwelleth in you?"

1 Corinthians 3:9, 10b, 16 (KJV)

Mercy:

"But the mercy of the Lord is from everlasting to everlasting upon them that fear him, and his righteousness unto children's children."

Psalms 103:17 (KJV)

Obedience:

"We ought to obey God rather than men."

Acts 5:29b (KJV)

Peace:

"Peace I leave with you, my peace I give unto you: not as the world giveth, give I unto you. Let not your heart be troubled, neither let it be afraid."

John 14:27 (KJV)

"And all thy children shall be taught of the Lord; and great shall be the peace of thy children."

Isaiah 54:13 (KJV)

Promise:

"What man is he that feareth the Lord? Him shall he teach in the way that he shall choose. His soul shall dwell at ease; and his seed shall inherit the earth. The secret of the Lord is with them that fear him; and he will shew them his covenant."

Psalms 25:12-14 (KJV)

"As for me, this is my covenant with them, saith the Lord; My Spirit that is upon thee, and my words which I have put in thy mouth, shall not depart out of thy mouth, nor out of the mouth of thy seed, nor out of the mouth of thy seed's seed, saith the Lord, from henceforth and for ever."

Isaiah 59:21 (KJV)

"My covenant will I not break, nor alter the thing that is gone out of my lips."

Psalms 89:34 (KJV)

"But as many as received him, to them gave He power to become the sons of God, even to them that believe on his name."

John 1:12 (KJV)

Prosperity:

"Beloved, I wish above all things that thou mayest prosper and be in health, even as thy soul prospereth."

3 John 2 (KJV)

Protection:

"Behold, I give unto you power to tread on serpents and scorpions, and over all the power of the enemy: and nothing shall by any means hurt you."

Luke 10:19 (KJV)

"No weapon that is formed against thee shall prosper; and every tongue that shall rise against thee in judgment thou shalt condemn. This is the heritage of the servants of the Lord, and their righteousness is of me, saith the Lord."

Isaiah 54:17 (KJV)

"Therefore whosoever heareth these sayings of mine and doeth them, I will liken him unto a wise man, which built his house upon a rock: (the rock Christ Jesus) and the rain descended, and the floods came, and the winds blew, and beat upon that house; and it fell not: for it was founded upon a rock."

Matthew 7:24-25 (KJV)

"Yet in all these things we are more than conquerors through Him who loved us."

Romans 8:37

"When the enemy shall come in like a flood, the Spirit of the Lord shall lift up a standard against him."

Isaiah 59:19b (KJV)

"When thou passest through the waters, I will be with thee; and through the rivers, they shall not overflow thee: when thou walkest through the fire, thou shalt not be burned; neither shall the flame kindle upon thee."

Isaiah 43:2 (KJV)

"Submit yourselves therefore to God. Resist the devil, and he will flee from you."

James 4:7 (KJV)

"But thus saith the Lord, Even the captives of the mighty shall be taken away, and the prey of the terrible shall be delivered: for I will contend with him that contendeth with thee, and I will save thy children."

Isaiah 49:25 (KJV)

"If God be for us, who can be against us?"

Romans 8:31b (KJV)

"I will make darkness light before them, and crooked things straight. These things will I do unto them, and not forsake them."

Isaiah 42:16b (KJV)

"Ye are of God, little children, and have overcome them: because greater is he that is in you, than he that is in the world."

1 John 4:4 (KJV)

Provision:

"But seek ye first the Kingdom of God, and his righteousness; and all these things (the things you have need of) shall be added unto you."

Matthew 6:33 (KJV)

Salvation:

"He who overcomes, I will make him a pillar in the temple of My God, and he will not go out from it anymore; and I will write upon him the name of My God, and the name of the city of My God, the new Jerusalem, which comes down out of heaven from My God, and I will write on him My new name."

Revelation 3:12 (NASB)

"If we confess our sins, he is faithful and just to forgive us our sins, and to cleanse us from all unrighteousness."

1 John 1:9 (KJV)

"Let him know, that he which converteth the sinner from the error of his way shall save a soul from death, and shall hide a multitude of sins."

James 5:20 (KJV)

Strength:

"Thy shoes shall be iron and brass; and as thy days, so shall thy strength be."

Deuteronomy 33:25 (KJV)

"He giveth power to the faint; and to them that have no might he increaseth strength. Even the youths shall faint and be weary, and the young men shall utterly fall: but they that wait upon the Lord shall renew their strength; they shall mount up with wings as eagles; they shall run, and not be weary; and they shall walk, and not faint."

Isaiah 40:29-31 (KJV)

Wisdom:

"If any of you lack wisdom, let him ask of God, that giveth to all men liberally, and upbraideth not; and it shall be given him. But let him ask in faith, nothing wavering."

James 1:5-6a (KJV)

"This Book of the Law shall not depart from your mouth, but you shall meditate in it day and night, that you may observe to do according to all that is written in it. For then you will make your way prosperous, and then you will have good success."

Joshua 1:8

(Our) Words:

"For by thy words thou shalt be justified, and by thy words thou shalt be condemned."

Matthew 12:37 (KJV)

"I create the fruit of the lips . . ."

Isaiah 57:19a (KJV)

"Whoso keepeth his mouth and his tongue keepeth his soul from troubles."

Proverbs 21:23 (KJV)

"There is that speaketh like the piercings of a sword: but the tongue of the wise is health."

Proverbs 12:18 (KJV)

"Seeing then that we have a great high priest, that is passed into the heavens, Jesus the Son of God, let us hold fast our profession (confession)."

Hebrews 4:14 (KJV)

"Death and life are in the power of the tongue: and they that love it shall eat the fruit thereof."

Proverbs 18:21 (KJV)

God bless you as you pray, build, and stand fast on His wonderful covenant promises!

Contact

Catheryne Wood

P. O. Box 29724

Dallas, Texas 75229

[info@catherynewood.org]

www.catherynewood.org

www.anarkfortodaysflood.org

Other Publications by Catheryne Wood

SEVEN LETTERS FROM JESUS

John the Baptist was sent to warn the people before Jesus' first coming, and these seven letters were sent through John the Apostle to warn the people before His second coming. In these letters, found in the Book of Revelation, Jesus instructs His Church what needs to be corrected to be ready for His soon return.

THE MYSTERIES OF 7 TRUTHS TWICE TOLD

The same "spiritual truths" Jesus taught in the parables of Matthew 13 are, again, brought out in His seven letters to the churches found in Revelation.

CPSIA information can be obtained at www.ICGtesting.com
Printed in the USA
LVOW092240281011

252500LV00002B/1/P